Floating
In
Florida

Floating

In

Florida

Discover 21 amazing adventures
on Florida's hidden waters

Lucy Beebe Tobias

ISBN (Paperback Edition)

979-8-218-40830-5

Library of Congress Control Number: 2024911651

Cover photo: Alan Youngblood/ Alan Youngblood Images. A glass bottom boat pulls in to be cleaned by the Silver Springs Professional Dive Team in the main springs at Silver Springs State Park, Ocala, Florida

Ten Thousand Island photo: Lorrie Muldowney

Jungle Queen photo: Jungle Queen Gallery

All other photos & illustrations: Lucy Beebe Tobias

Printed and bound in the United States of America

First printing September 2024

Published by Sea Aster Press, Sarasota, Florida

For my father, Robert Park Beebe, master mariner

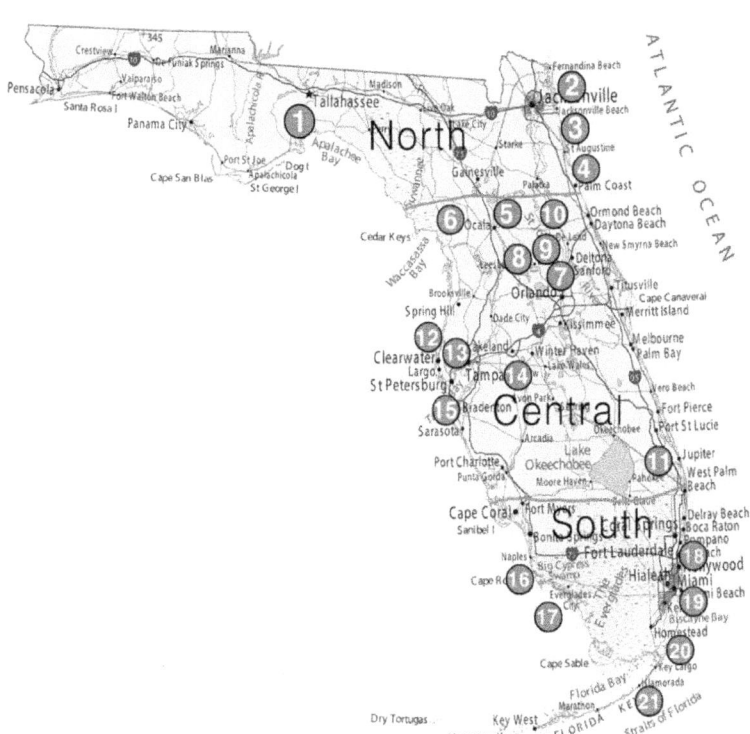

Contents

Introduction

North Florida

Central Florida

Introduction

A Florida boat tour is a short ride, usually two hours or less, where you and your fellow passengers learn something new about Florida history, ecology or wildlife from a spirited and helpful guide while gliding across supple, sun filled waters. You may see dolphins, manatees, turtles, alligators, and more. Cruise past famous and infamous homes, Indian mounds, and ancient cypress trees where diving birds sit on branches spreading their wings to let them dry. A boat tour is a floating adventure with friends.

Long before railroads and interstate highways, major rivers in Florida – the Kissimmee, St. Johns, Ocklawaha, Suwannee, Apalachicola, and Caloosahatchee – were the roads of choice for settlers. Ships docked at ports like Jacksonville, Key West, and Cedar Key, then goods were transferred to tall steamboats – narrow in beam with shallow flat draft – perfect for rivers and lakes.

Pontoon boats today have the same narrow beam and shallow flat draft as those 19th century river steamboats, making them just right for river, lake, bay and intracoastal waterway tours. There may be a bit of rocking from the wakes of passing boats, but most of the time, a river tour floats along smoothly.

Boarding a pontoon boat is easy, involving a short ramp or some steps. There is often a railing and always a crew member standing by to lend a helping hand getting aboard. Many, but not all, pontoon boats are also wheelchair accessible.

Boat tours are weather dependent. Some stick to the schedule, rain or shine, others do not. If lightening is nearby, rest assured tours are cancelled.

Boat trips and boat tours are different. A boat trip takes you from Point A to Point B, like the catamaran that speeds people from Fort Myers to Key West, or from Key West to the Dry Tortugas.

A boat tour, on the other hand, takes you from a dock out onto lakes and rivers, then brings you back to where you started, and not far from where you parked your car. The trip is your destination. Think of it as the ideal day outing. A short adventure, usually on a comfortable pontoon boat, and you are done in time for lunch, dinner, a latte, or cocktails.

Boat captains and mates represent authentic Florida. One example: The singing boat tour captain in Dunnellon grew up on the Rainbow and Withlacoochee Rivers. You will hear their own brand of humor, honed by personal experience.

All boat crews appreciate tips. Look for a container near where you boarded the boat. Often passengers can bring their own food and drinks (alcoholic and non-alcoholic). Usually, bottled water is for sale on the boat. If you want to bring your leashed dog aboard, check the boat tour website ahead of time to see if pets are welcome. Also, boat tour times and prices are subject to change. Call ahead for current rates and tour times.

Floating in Florida takes you to tested, easy excursions that will educate, entertain, and bring a smile to your face. In this guidebook you will find twenty-one different boat tours, a generous sampling that will have you, your family and friends discovering features of Florida that you might not know existed. Enjoy them all.

North
Florida

6

Chapter 1

Jungle Cruise Tour

Duration: 45 minutes

Cost: $7.44 adults, call for all prices.

Park admission also required.

Location: 550 Wakulla Park Drive,

Wakulla Springs, FL

Phone: 855-632-4559

Website

https://thelodgeatwakullasprings.com/boat-tour/

Good to know: Reservations required.

Wheelchair accessible boats and a manual

Wheelchair available on request

The jungle cruise at Edward Ball Wakulla Springs State Park floats visitors one mile down the Wakulla River and one mile back plus a loop around the famous Wakulla Springs, one of the largest freshwater springs in the world, discharging 250 million gallons of water a day. The flow coming out of 32 underwater caves could fill an Olympic size swimming pool every few minutes.

For everyone aboard, the biggest treat of this boat tour is the world class wildlife viewing. All heads on board swivel back and forth, trying to take it all in. So much wildlife! There is a reason for this. Our boat captain and park ranger Collin Johnson explains. Inside the park the first three miles of the river are restricted to boat tours only.

Hooded mergansers floating on the river surface decide they want to fly. Takeoff is a noisy process. Their wings flap, their feet slap the water, leaving pops of water spray as they skim over the surface of the Wakulla River trying to gain altitude. Finally, liftoff! All this accompanied by lots of vocalization.

Common gallinules bob on the surface of nearby marshes, unperturbed by the mergansers' takeoff antics. Gallinules are attractive marsh birds with charcoal grey bodies, bright red forehead shields and red bills graced by a touch of bright yellow on the tips, as though they dipped their bills in yellow paint.

Leafless bald cypress trees are generously draped with Spanish moss. The trees, that can be hundreds of years old, flourish along the shoreline and in the middle

of the river. These trees provide perches for curlews, with their white bodies and orange curved beaks.

The anhinga, seen on branches drying its wings or in the water, is a water bird that swims like a snake and flies like a turkey, thus they are often called snake birds or water turkeys. The tree branches also accommodate cormorants drying their wings along with black vultures waiting quietly for their next meal. Our boat captain calls vultures "nature's cleanup crew." They are migratory. Somehow that information is comforting.

Rafts of river grasses become beds for alligators. Lots of alligators. Big ones. Little ones. Medium sized ones. Sunning themselves. Storing energy in their bodies so they can go swimming through the night looking for prey.

Take a deep breath and observe what is NOT there. No other boats, no docks, no canoes, no kayaks, no human habitation, no logging, no houses, no people except in the swimming area at Wakulla Springs. Wildlife has a chance to live undisturbed. And they are doing just that, in abundance.

Before the pontoon boat even leaves the dock for the jungle cruise, Johnson opens a guitar case, tunes a guitar, and tells us he has written songs about the river. Then he sings to us! Puts the guitar away, unties the boat lines, and off we go. Marvelous.

The Wakulla River flows for 9 miles, emptying into the St. Marks River, three miles long, then all pouring into Apalachicola Bay and the Gulf of Mexico. Wakulla Springs is located 14 miles south of Tallahassee, Florida.

In the restricted part of the river the flora and fauna are so spectacular and feel so ancient. No wonder this area was the setting, both underwater and above, for an early Tarzan movie, *Tarzan's Secret Treasure*, which debuted in 1941.

Tarzan's Secret Treasure was supposed to be set in Africa. Wakulla Springs was the substitute. The movie company even managed to bring in an elephant. That was a feat! Our captain says Johnny Weissmuller perfected his Tarzan cry right here, on the river. He also had a fight scene with an army of alligators.

One area on the river is called Tarzan's Island and has bare trees full of turkey vultures. They sit hunched, silent, and staring at the pontoon boat and its occupants, who stare back. Just a tad too ghoulish for me, but still another example of wildlife flourishing here.

The state of Florida bought Wakulla Springs, which includes the Wakulla Lodge, in the 1980s. There is a restaurant inside the Lodge that is open to the public.

Jungle cruise boats and check in area are located behind the Lodge. Four tour boats are tied up to the dock, ready to go.

My boat tour

Date _____

_____

_____

_____

_____

Chapter 2

Cumberland Coastal Tour, Amelia
River Cruises, Fernandina Beach

Duration: 90 minutes

Cost: Adults $30, children $24, seniors $28

Location: 1 N. Front St., Fernandina Beach,
FL

Phone: 904-261-9972

Website: https://ameliarivercruises.com

Good to know: Reservations recommended

Arrive thirty minutes early. Search for a parking place at the Fernandina Harbor Marina located at the foot of Centre Street. Found one? Great. You are golden for the whole day. There is also parking on Centre Street and side streets of historic downtown Fernandina Beach, all within walking distance of the dock. Parking is free.

Check in at the Amelia River Cruises ticket kiosk. It is the small white building on the dock. Even though your reservation was confirmed ahead of time, you still need a boarding pass. Their tours are popular. Reservations recommended.

Boarding is promptly on time. Boarding passes collected then. A long slightly sloping boat ramp to the dock and another ramp to board. Seats are bus style, and both sides are good — coming and going offer the same view to each side, everyone gets a good look at Amelia River, Cumberland Sound, Cumberland River, and Cumberland Island.

Captain Kurt goes through the drill — pointing out to passengers where the life jackets are located. This is mandatory on every boat tour and happens before leaving the dock.

He also talks trash. Passenger's trash. Sea turtles, he says, eat plastic bags, mistaking them for jelly fish, their favorite food. The bags stick in their stomachs, and they die. Passengers are urged to place all trash in the trash can at the back of the boat. No trash overboard.

Then a bit of Captain humor: "Anyone missing someone from their group? Anyone wishing someone from their group was missing?"

Casting off, the captain outlines some of what we will, and might see — the Atlantic Ocean, Fort Clinch State Park, manatees, sea turtles, sea birds, wild horses, and historic homes.

Fernandina Beach is the only place in the United States to have been under eight flags — French, Spanish, British, pirates (several times) and the United States. This town has the nickname of being the back door to the United States. When there was an embargo, ships came here to unload. Easy access from the Atlantic Ocean.

David Yulee dreamed of connecting the two Florida coasts by railroad. It took him from 1844 to 1861 to get 154 miles of track finished from Fernandina to Cedar Key. European goods arrived by ship then transported across the state by train. Loaded on another ship in Cedar Key, destinations became available all over the Gulf of Mexico.

A north/south railroad connected with Yulee's. Produce came from up north packed in ice, lots of ice. So much so that Fernandina built an icehouse. For the first time, with all that ice, locally caught shrimp could be shipped up north. The shrimp industry soared. Ice made the difference.

And so did otter trawl nets. Added to shrimp boats in the early 1900s, the trawl nets allowed shrimpers to net along the bottom. The very first year they were used, our captain tells us, three million pounds of shrimp landed on the docks.

Of the 140 shrimp boats that were once here, most are gone in large part due to the growth of shrimp farms in the 1970s. But Fernandina's shrimping history is not forgotten. Every May there is a Shrimp Festival complete with a parade, craft shows, music, food and, you guessed it, shrimp by the bucketful.

Our tour boat floats past a shrimp boat, not currently being used, that has trawl nets. The captain points to turtle extruder doors, added in the 1960s because of environmental concerns for turtles. Loggerhead turtles would get caught in the trawl nets and drown. The doors give them an escape hatch.

It is impossible to miss the two large paper mills, one on either side of Fernandina Beach. Owned by Rayonier, the mills have been operating for over 85 years, making craft paper. Logs arrive, twenty-four hours a day, and are turned into wood chips that then become craft paper that is shipped to Georgia.

The wood chip piles are so high we all must look up at these mini pyramids as we cruise by. For every tree cut down four more are planted. Trees come from Florida and Georgia. Rayonier is the second largest landowner in Florida behind the state itself.

Looking away from land out over the river, the captain points to Tiger Island, also known as Snake Island. So many snakes. He tells passengers all snakes can swim. Seriously? Oh dear.

On our right side is a high bluff, known as Old Town, the original settlement, still there today with many historic homes visible from the water. When the train tracks were laid in the 1800s, the town moved down to flat land along the Amelia River and that became downtown historic Fernandina Beach.

Our tour boat leaves Amelia River and comes to Cumberland Sound. We cross the invisible divide between Florida and Georgia. Cheers. Fort Clinch is on the Florida side, Cumberland Island on the Georgia side.

This is called the St. Marys entrance to Cumberland Sound and is used by Ohio class submarines coming and going from the Naval Submarine Base Kings Bay, St. Marys, Georgia.

As soon as the marsh lands of Cumberland Island are close, all eyes are peeled for sightings of wild horses. We are not disappointed. A large brown horse is standing in the marshes, and we will see more horses as we float along the edge of the island.

Since 1972 most of the island has been under the umbrella of the National Park Service and known as

Cumberland Island National Seashore. But in the 1800s, this island was a playground for rich industrialists, particularly the Chandler and Carnegie families. One family member, Lucy Carnegie Ricketson Ferguson (1899-1989) had nine children and some three hundred servants. She worked hard during her life to conserve Cumberland Island. In her will, she wanted her 40 horses set free on the island. Two of those horses were ungelded white stallions she purchased from the last emperor of Russia. That is why there are some white horses on the island mixed in with all the others.

Photo albums of the families that used to live on Cumberland Island and events are passed around. Today some thirty-seven people live on the island and half of those work at Greyfield Inn, built by the Carnegies in 1890 and still open for business. John F. Kennedy Jr. and Carolyn Bessette stayed at Greyfield Inn when they came to Cumberland Island to be married in a secret ceremony on September 21, 1996.

Reaching the turnaround point about halfway up Cumberland Island, the boat turns, picks up speed and heads back to Fernandina. The captain says his narration is over and enjoy the ride. A group of ten or so women pass around a vodka bottle. Glasses are raised. By the time we return to the dock, the bottle is empty.

My boat tour

Date _____

_____

_____

_____

_____

Chapter 3

Red Boat Dolphin Odyssey &
Sightseeing Tour

Duration: 90 minutes

Cost: $29, call for all costs

Phone: 904-436-3566

Location: Vilano Fishing Pier, 260 Vilano
Road, Vilano Beach, FL

Website: https://redboattours.com

Good to know: Family friendly. All ages
welcome. No pets of any kind except
registered service dogs and bring their papers.
Handicapped accessible

The Red Boat Tour is still tied up to the floating dock
and already Captain James has spotted dolphins. He
suggests we all look up on the Vilano Fishing Pier. Yep.
Dolphins. Three of them in flight, sculptures on the pier.
Passengers laugh. We're off to a good start.

Captain James reminds his audience that we are in fact going out on the water and may or may not see wildlife. But chances are good. Some 200 documented dolphins live in the Intracoastal Waterway, and most are in family pods. Lucky for us the Red Boat Dolphin Odyssey is aptly named. The crew knows where to find dolphins.

This brand new red boat is family owned and operated by Captain Tony and Miss Jennifer Patesotti.

Today's crew, Captain James, and First Mate Tony, call themselves stand-ins for Tony and Jennifer.

The red boat is built pontoon style with a covered top featuring seating down both sides and a row of seats down the middle. Ample room for everyone. Today's boat tour has a mixture of families with young children, and vacationers of varied ages. Younger kids, total strangers, quickly gravitate to each other, sitting down on the deck and sharing toys they brought with them. They'll jump up when a dolphin is sighted then go back to playing.

At an inlet that opens onto the Atlantic Ocean, the captain reminds us that the Atlantic Ocean is 4,000 miles wide. Should we make the passage, North Africa is on the other side along with Morocco and the Canary Islands.

Floating slowly past Anastasia State Park, the view is sandy beaches with scrub and trees. This is a more remote part of the park, a walk to get here, which could explain why we are not seeing people on the beach.

A dorsal fin of a dolphin appears out of the water and passengers of all ages get excited, standing, cell phones ready for the next sighting. True confession: All my photos just show green water, never did capture a dolphin fin however it was fun trying.

Dolphins come up often to breathe. But their main business is eating. An adult dolphin needs to eat forty pounds of fish a day. All dolphin dorsal fins are different. They are not tagged but the fins are identified by their characteristics, and all are in a database.

Seeing just one dolphin, the captain suggests it is a young male. Dolphins are family oriented, young dolphins and their parents living in pods, but when a young male gets ready "to look at other dolphins" to use the captain's quote, the pod kicks him out and he is on his own to find another pod.

Passengers are encouraged to look for two bald eagles that like to hang out in the dead trees at Anastasia State Park but today they are not to be seen. We keep an eagle eye out anyway.

Another reason people are not to be seen along the sandy shores of the state park – there are snakes, lots of snakes. Wearing shoes and long trousers encouraged.

In the water, just head and long neck sticking out, is a double breasted cormorant. This one is wild and free. In China, the captain relates, cormorants are part of fishing families. A ring is put around their neck to keep them from swallowing fish. A string is attached to one leg. Then the cormorant is sent down into the water to catch fish, small ones, some four to six inches long. The fisherman gets the first four fish, the fifth fish goes to the cormorant. Presumably the ring is removed for dinnertime.

The red boat floats towards the St. Augustine lighthouse, standing 165 feet tall with a bold black and white stripe pattern up the sides, an observation deck and red top. We're told some serious local runners run up the 219 stairs to the observation deck every morning. Sounds exhausting.

Allegedly this is a very haunted lighthouse. The Ghost Hunters have been here twice. The captain assures us that if it has been on YouTube it must be true. Laughter. Heads nod.

Every lighthouse has a different pattern to distinguish it during the day. At night each light has a different light pattern, and it can be seen twenty miles out to sea. If mariners have charts or books with these patterns, they can identify where they are.

It is so fine to be out on the water, cut loose from land, to be a passenger not the pilot, with just simple chores – looking for dolphins and admiring the shoreline, the park, houses, marinas, ancient buildings downtown.

Yet, as the saying goes, there is trouble in paradise. The captain notes 1000 people a month are moving into St. Johns County. Traffic is becoming unbearable. This information, and the truth of traffic congestion in our lives, is another reason it feels so relaxing to be out on the water.

There is water traffic – kayaks, paddleboards, small skiffs, mid-size trawlers, fishing boats, a steady parade going both ways on the Intracoastal. Some slow down when dolphins are sighted, others go by at high speed, oblivious, throwing tall wakes called rooster tails.

Nearer to shore, we approach the Bridge of Lions, started in 1925 and finished in 1927. The bridge connects downtown St. Augustine to Anastasia Island across Matanzas Bay. Our captain points out the two lions guarding the St. Augustine end of the bridge. They are famous copies of the marble Medici lion, made of Carrara marble from the same quarry in Tuscany, Italy used by Michelangelo.

Next up on the shoreline is the Castillo de San Marcos, which took 23 years to build out of native coquina stone. As part of reenactments, cannons are fired periodically but we glide by without a shot across the bow.

Then a huge cross comes into view, marking the spot where Spanish soldier Pedro Menendez de Aviles in 1565 landed eleven ships with 2200 soldiers. All aboard went ashore, met the very tall Timucuan Indians and the first mass was said. St. Augustine is the oldest permanent European settlement in what is now the United States.

The previous cross was demolished by Hurricane Dora in 1964. A new cross rose up in the sky in 1965, made of seventy tons of stainless steel. Concrete was poured thirty feet into the ground. Worked. Cross is still standing today.

First Mate Roy hands every person a fancy sticker saying, "I saw a dolphin" Red Boat Tours. Naturally, the young kids get two or three stickers each, applying them to clothing, bare knees, their toys. All in all, a good day.

My boat tour

Date _____

_____

_____

_____

_____

Chapter 4

> St. Augustine Scenic Cruise
>
> Duration: 75 minutes
>
> Cost: Adults, $24.50, seniors (60+) $21.00,
>
> Children (4-12) $11.00
>
> Phone: 800-542-8316
>
> Location: 111 Avenida Menendez, St.
>
> Augustine, FL
>
> Website: https://scenic-cruise.com/
>
> Good to know: Not handicapped accessible.

The Victory III scenic boat tour is easily accessible at the St. Augustine Municipal Marina. It is also the location of the tour's ticket office. The marina sits just south of the Bridge of Lions at the heart of downtown historic St. Augustine. All parking around the marina is metered street parking.

This scenic tour, started by the Usina family, has floated along in a line of different boats since the 1900s

– making it the oldest scenic tour in St. Augustine. They started with ferrying supplies to the island of Vilano before the bridge was built and eventually became full time sightseeing tours. The current double decker vessel, Victory III, with the top deck open, is easily spotted at its marina mooring.

Tied up nearby is a replica of Magellan's ship that sailed around the world from 1519 to 1522. Built in Spain, visitors can take tours on board. Our captain points out the Magellan ship, and recommends their tour, as we get ready to depart. The whistle blows. We cast off.

The cash bar opens for business serving beer, wine, bottled water, and small snacks. Passengers can bring non-alcoholic beverages but no alcoholic beverages. Good to know: two restrooms on board.

Passengers already appreciate the fact that the Ancient City is ancient, but still it comes as a surprise to learn St. Augustine was founded in 1565, a full fifty-five years before pilgrims landed on Plymouth Rock. It is the oldest continuously occupied settlement of European and African American origin in the United States.

Our captain continues his narration, saying we may see dolphins, and we do, but it is too early to see loggerhead turtles. Nesting season is about to start. A reminder that what passengers see on a tour depends in part on the time of year.

Floating close to Anastasia State Park, the captain recalls his teenage years growing up in St. Augustine. He and friends would visit the island, capture rattlesnakes, take them to what is now known as the St. Augustine Alligator Farm Zoological Park and sell the snakes to Ross Allan, who milked the snakes for their venom.

A few years go by. Researchers at Anastasia noticed a huge increase in the rat population. When staff was asked for a reason, they suggested it could be because local teenagers captured snakes and sold them. So, the practice was stopped. Snakes rebounded. Rats decreased.

A group of pelicans fly overhead in V formation then swoop down and glide low over the water, looking for fish. Dolphins come up to the surface to breathe. A cormorant sits on a piling drying its wings. I'm sitting in the bow on the ground level and have a great panoramic view.

We float by the St. Augustine Lighthouse and Maritime Museum at Ponce Inlet. Standing 175 feet tall, its light shines twenty miles out into the Atlantic Ocean. The first wooden lighthouse was built in the 1500s. More lighthouses followed and lighthouse keepers used to live next to the lighthouse. There is a lot of history here. Our captain recommends visiting and taking one of their tours like the Keeper's Tour or the Dark of the Moon Ghost Tour.

My scenic boat tour takes place late afternoon on a fine spring day. It is the last tour of the day. I recommend checking their website for tours year round. The times and availability change.

Also check their website, or call, for times for the Nights of Lights cruises. From November through January millions of tiny lights illuminate the Ancient City. It is a sight to see, especially from the water. The boat itself will also be decked out with lots of lights. These nights of lights tours are immensely popular. Rightly so. Book in advance.

Why all the lights? Historically, way back before electricity, when ships were out in the ocean fishing, families waiting in St. Augustine placed a single lighted candle in every window of the house to await returning ships. The mariners out at sea could see all the twinkling lights. That and the lighthouse light guided them home.

My boat tour

Date _____

_____

_____

_____

_____

Central Florida

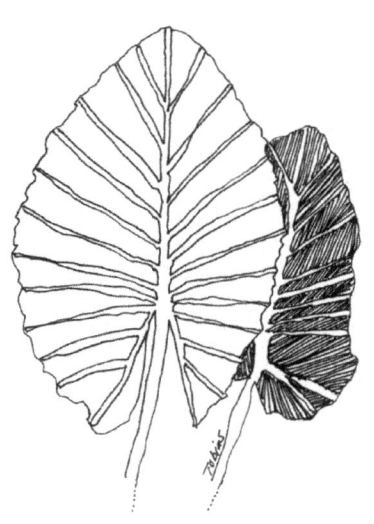

Chapter 5

Glass Bottomed Boat Tour

Duration: 30 minutes or 90 minutes

Cost: $14 to $30 depending on tour

Plus $2 park entrance fee per person

Location: Silver Springs State Park,

5656 East Silver Springs Blvd., Ocala, FL

Phone: 352-261-5840

Website: https://silversprings.com

Good to know: one boat in fleet of nine is

wheelchair accessible – Chief Potachee,

select time slot for wheelchair accessible

Imagine sitting in a pontoon boat looking down through a glass bottom at river life below – fish swim by, a turtle or two, maybe a manatee. Eel grass sways in the current dancing to a melody only eel grass can hear. Above water birds rest on tree limbs. Alligators sun themselves on fallen logs.

Silver Springs is the largest artesian spring area in the world, discharging some 500 million gallons of water a day. Along with other springs, it feeds into the Silver River. Glass bottomed boats have been floating down the river and wowing visitors since the 1870s, making it perhaps the oldest attraction in Florida.

My family is one of those wowed over the years by this boat ride.

At an early age, my parents brought me to Silver Springs. We went on the glass bottomed boat ride, looking down at the underwater world. Eel grass swayed with the current. Huge catfish looked up at us as we floated by overhead. Big gar with long snouts swam underneath us. I was enchanted.

Years later, married with children, I brought my three boys to Silver Springs. We took the glass bottomed boat ride. They loved it.

Today taking a glass bottomed boat ride still goes on. Land on both sides of the river is managed by Silver Springs State Park. There are two rides, a 30 minute ride and a 90 minute ride. A friend and I opted for the 90 minute ride. Reservations are highly recommended as both rides are very popular.

Joining a line waiting in a covered pavilion, tickets in hand, the wait is not long. Boarding is simple and quick. Passengers include families with young children, teenagers, couples, seniors and even a couple of visitors from foreign lands. The captain asks for a show of hands from those who have been on a glass bottomed boat tour before – more than half raise their hands.

A bench lines each side of the glass bottomed boat. Both benches fill up fast. The pontoon boat engine is electric – quiet – making it easy to hear our tour guide who is also the boat captain. The boat dock is located at the largest artesian spring, but our tour guide saves that for last. And so, we start down the river, passing over smaller springs. The boat slows so we can see bubbles coming up out of the sand – a small spring water gushing up from deep underground. Fish gather around the opening.

Quite a few fish also gather under the boat. Of course. Boat equals food. The captain tosses out some fish food pellets. Look closely and see there is already fish food in the water! From previous boats. No hungry fish here. The boat glides on to the next spring.

Coming up the river towards us is a flotilla of canoes, kayaks, and paddleboards. It is a parade. Everyone dressed in Christmas garb. Our captain tells us a boat club puts on this Christmas water parade every year. And we are lucky. Today is the day.

Also on the water are kayaks made of clear plastic, so you see what is going on underwater – very cool. I had not seen one of these before, only heard about them. Gliding along, our captain reels off a long list of movies and television shows, all doing underwater scenes right here on the Silver River, in the artesian springs.

Going upstream are two boats filled with divers. They are researchers studying the river.

Along both sides of the river are a treasure trove of trees – some bare, it is late fall, and some showing their fall colors – leaves of gold, brown, orange, russet, and red. Beautiful.

A manatee and her calf are spotted resting in the shallows. Already a cluster of canoes and kayaks are gathering in a semi-circle around them. Our pontoon boat approaches slowly and stays at a respectful distance, so as not to stress the manatees.

It is never a guarantee that on a boat tour something amazing like a manatee will be seen. This is special and the whole boat knows it.

Returning up the river, our tour boat makes a slow circle around the Silver Springs. Statues from a long ago film still lay in the water. A cave opening on one side has also been used in movie scenes.

Tying up at the dock, everyone disembarks. Will we be back? Yes. Taking this ride is a tradition. It never gets old, only better.

My boat tour

Date _____

_____

_____

_____

_____

Chapter 6

> ## Singing River Tour, Dunnellon
>
> Duration: 90 minutes
>
> Cost: $20 cash
>
> Location: Dunnellon City Boat Ramp, 20750 River Drive, Dunnellon, FL
>
> Phone: 352-804-1573
>
> Website: https://www.singingrivertours.com
>
> Good to know: Reservations required and made by phone only. Handicapped accessible

Jon Semmes is both a professional boat captain and musician. His 40-foot pontoon boat is spotlessly clean and sports a covered top. Passengers sit along both sides leaving the center open for Jon to walk up and down conveying river facts without having to use a microphone.

The Singing River Tour combines an eco-tour with original music. It is a pleasurable partnership. On the day

I arrived the weather was picture perfect — sunshine, no wind, blue sky. A ramp with no incline made boarding easy. Jon thanks passengers for being prompt to arrive, the ramp is removed, a line is cast off and our floating trip begins on the Withlacoochee River.

The water is dark, a deep tea color, a result of tannic acid made from an abundance of leaves falling in the river. Imagine a tea bag sitting way too long in a teacup. That is the color of the water. It is impossible to see the bottom.

But a change happens abruptly. At the confluence where the Withlacoochee River meets the Rainbow River, the water goes from dark Withlacoochee tannic acid color to the clear water showing sandy bottom and sea grass of the Rainbow River. Unusual. Dramatic. Floating on dark water one moment, clear water the next, a sharp divide, like a heavy velvet stage curtain, between the two.

Jon points out American coots, snowbirds who only show up in the winter, floating nearby, unimpressed by this water change where rivers meet. A solitary wood stork sits on a lawn of a riverfront home, while a cormorant perches on a dock.

One side of the Rainbow has cypress trees decked with Spanish moss, live oaks, sweet gum, and water oaks. Some trees are still winter bare, others are dressed in a new coat of bright spring green leaves. The other side has houses, lawns sloping to the water, and quite a few double decker docks — boats tied up on the water level, a porch for sitting on the top level.

In-between drawing passengers' attention to birds, otters, and alligators and pointing out local history along the way, like the home on the Rainbow River where he grew up, Jon shares Florida's water story.

Rain falls. It takes 12 to 15 years for that rain to percolate down into the Floridan Aquifer and then bubble up in springs. The Rainbow River is completely spring fed. There are 750 spring fed rivers in Florida, more than any other place in the world. Wow! But springs face trouble.

Water levels are getting lower as Florida's population soars to twenty-three million, and everyone tries to keep their lawns green all year, using vast quantities water and fertilizer, like it was up north. Jon points out using less water and fertilizer would help the very river we are floating on to survive. This produces nervous laughter among passengers. It is a tall order, a changing of mindset.

One spring Jon mentions gets 400 million gallons of water a day from the Floridan Aquifer— about what the city of Tampa uses every day. And while 400 million sounds like a lot, the same spring pumped out 600 million gallons of water a day ten years ago. Ninety percent of all water used in Florida comes from the Floridan Aquifer and it is being pulled out before it reaches the springs.

The Withlacoochee River— the name means crooked river – starts in the Green Swamp, the second largest wetlands in Florida, right behind the Everglades.

Our pontoon boat floats along on the Rainbow River, gliding on the very spring fed water that makes Florida unique. It is both endangered and beautiful at the same time.

On this picture perfect day, wading birds are everywhere. An American egret stands tall in a bed of what looks like water lettuce. Nearby there are white ibis with long curved red beaks. Jon points out a pair of nesting sand hill cranes, pied-billed grebes, and a small tri-colored heron.

One section of the Rainbow River has numerous wooded boxes on poles above the water line. These are nesting boxes for wood ducks.

A great blue heron stands watch in the shallows.

It was a surprise to learn from Jon this big bird has very light bones, weighs less than two pounds and can live up to twenty years of age.

Several logs exposed above the water are lined with turtles, crammed together head and tails touching, sunning themselves. Jon identifies them as Florida basking turtles. They lounge around very well. An example to us all.

While the University of Florida's mascot is a green alligator, the real thing, an adult alligator, is not green but a deep slate gray. It is hard for the untrained eye to spot alligators, but Jon sees them, usually half out of the water sunning themselves and the boat nudges in for a closer look.

When the time comes for singing, the pilot turns off the engine and the boat rests in a bed of river plants. Jon gets out his guitar and sings three songs about wild Florida, written by locals. The third song was written by his mother, about her son growing up to be a Florida man — one passionate and committed to this place, its ecosystems, beauty, and challenges.

A personal note: It took me three tries to take this tour! First two times Jon cancelled due to weather forecast, once for rain predicted all day, once for a hurricane watch. Uh oh. So glad I persisted. A wonderful day on the water.

The Dunnellon City Boat Ramp is located behind City Hall. Free parking in the City Hall lot — it was a Saturday for my tour so any spot would do — then a short walk down a paved slope to the dock on the Withlacoochee River.

My boat tour

Date _____

Chapter 7

Scenic Boat Tour

Duration: 60 minutes

Cost: $16 adults, $8 children (2-11)

Location: 312 E. Morse Blvd., Winter Park, FL

Phone: 407-644-4056

Website: https://www.scenicboattours.com

Good to know: First come, first served

Scenic boat tours began on a chain of lakes in Winter Park, Florida, in 1938. They were an instant hit then and remain quite popular today.

Six pontoon boats carry 18 passengers each. Arrive early, get a ticket, take a seat in a covered waiting area. This is a first come, first served boat tour.

Each tour starts off by churning across Lake Osceola then puttering slowly along Fern Canal. During the 12 mile boat tour we visit three lakes and two canals.

Everyone ducks their heads going under a low canal bridge in Fern Canal. Our Captain, Tom Smith, informs us we now know the reason why there are no canopies on the pontoon boats—low bridges.

Having no boat canopy provides you with a good reason to bring a hat (preferably one with a tie down as the pontoon boats can pick up speed going across a lake). Also advised: carry with you or buy water there. Consider sunscreen or wearing long sleeved shirt.

On my trip we were told Winter Park was under a heat advisory. It was a 93 degree summer day. The heat index made it feel like 103 degrees. Everyone had water. Everyone was willing to give it a go.

To me, the canals were both a saving grace and surprisingly unique part of the trip.

Narrow, with intimate looks at back gardens on both sides, canal edges are heavily landscaped and full of lush surprises.

We looked up at a tall banana tree loaded with ripening bananas, floated past cypress trees, ferns, an ancient oak tree, 150 years old according to Captain Smith, and saw wildly beautiful tropical flowers.

Cameras clicked continuously. No matter where you sit in the pontoon boat the view is great. The canals are all old growth landscape with tall trees, lots of shade.

When entering a lake, Captain Smith kicked up the speed – we had to hold onto our hats. Going fast has the added benefit of providing a cooling effect.

Then he'd slow down for points of interest—much of the Rollins College campus touches the water's edge on Lake Virginia. Smith points out the college chapel tower standing high above other buildings.

The college's ski team has waterfront space. A large jumping ramp, pulled to shore during the summer, will be put out in the lake for training during the school year.

We puttered by many large homes including a humongous house under construction. When finished, Smith tells us, it will have 45,000 square feet. Whoa. Then we idle by a home purchased by Mister Rogers' parents. Yes, that Mister Rogers. Fred Rogers' parents bought the lakeside home to be nearer their son who was studying musical composition at Rollins College.

That piece of history surprised me. I always thought of Mister Rogers as stepping into a brownstone house on a busy urban street, in a metropolitan area, taking off his shoes, hanging up his coat. Ah, no matter where he was, it was a beautiful day in the neighborhood.

On the Rollins College campus near the chapel there is a Mister Rogers sculpture called *A Beautiful Day for a Neighbor* by British sculptor Paul Day. And right near that sculpture is a labyrinth. No, a labyrinth is not a maze. You cannot get lost. This is an easy, meditative walk on an easy path to the center and out again.

Captain Smith tells us if we have the time, Knowles Memorial Chapel, built between 1931-1932 on the Rollins College campus, is worth a visit. Try the front door. If open, go inside, lots to see including a beautiful circular stained glass window.

At noon every day the bell hanging in the chapel bell tower rings. It is the same bell that called students to class on that first day of classes in 1886. Awesome.

Chapel, labyrinth, sculpture, a cluster close to each other at Rollins College. Could this be a plan for after the boat tour? Maybe return on a cooler day.

All the lakes have homes facing water. A few are old, as in a century or more. But most are new—tear down the old house and build something bigger on the site. One home that someone wanted to save was cut in half and the halves transported to another lakeside site and reassembled.

On every lake and intracoastal water tour I've taken, the narration, whether historical or contemporary, has a bit of a gossipy feel, as if ripped from the pages of tell all magazines. And this ride is no exception.

Captain Smith comes close to shore to show us the Albin Polasek Museum and Sculpture Gardens. Polasek, a prolific and prominent sculptor, retired to Winter Park in 1950, building a Mediterranean style home on Lake Osceola and marrying one of his former students. He was 71. She was 61. It was a first marriage for both.

Today you can tour the gardens and home, self-guided or with a docent. The Gardens are a popular venue for weddings. And artists.

Every year the town of Winter Park sponsors a Paint Out. A check of the Paint Out website will provide future dates and happenings. There are free painting demonstrations around town. Some of the plein aire artists set up their easels at Albin Polasek Museum and Sculpture Gardens.

I'm a big believer in destination bundling. Look at a calendar. Plan a multi-day excursion to Winter Park that includes a boat tour and stay for the Paint Out. Visit Rollins College. Go to the Saturday Farmers Market. Stay at the Alfond Inn, a boutique inn right next to Rollins College.

Include a visit to the Charles Hosmer Morse Museum of American Art with the largest collection anywhere of work by Charles Morse and Louis Comfort Tiffany. Check to see if the Morse still has free admission on Friday nights.

And now let us address the bane of car travel. That would be parking. Does it exist in Winter Park? Street parking fills up quickly. By the time I arrived around 10:30 am for the 11 am. boat tour on a Saturday, all spaces along Park Avenue were gone.

I tried not to panic. Turning off Park Avenue onto Morse Blvd, a dead end street with the boat tour dock at the end, I saw a few open spaces close to the water. Grabbed one. Felt relieved. Parking karma. Sometimes it works. And it gets better. These spaces have up to three hours. Free.

After the one hour boat tour, my free parking space was still good for two hours. I walked up the hill to Park Avenue, a true shopping buffet in both directions. And faithful to its street name, there is a lovely park on the other side of the street. This is where the Saturday Farmers Market takes place. The train station is here too.

Ah, possibilities. But I'm feeling languid, not in a hurry. A lovely boat trip does that for you. Slows things down. Makes you want to look around. Be amazed. Enjoy the moment.

My boat tour

Date _____

_____

_____

_____

Chapter 8

> ## Dora Canal Tour, Mount Dora
>
> Duration: Two hours tour at 11 am and 2 pm
>
> Cost: $35 adults (call for all price ranges)
>
> Location: 100 North Alexander Street,
>
> Mount Dora, FL
>
> Phone: 352-434-8040
>
> Website: https://www.doracanaltour.com
>
> Good to know: Reservations required.
>
> Walkers and wheelchairs welcome. No
>
> scooters or power wheelchairs

Lake Dora spreads out before us, a gigantic round bowl filled with murky water. Trees and homes rim the bowl. Our pontoon boat skims across the water. We pass a group of double-breasted cormorants floating together in a clump. They are not perturbed by us.

Before casting off from the dock at Lakeside Inn, clipboards were passed around with a game. A bingo shaped card has all kinds of names, instead of numbers, names like anhinga, cormorant, even reindeer (we'll get to that later). You put an X for every one of the names seen.

Premier Boat Tours has two covered pontoon boats with plastic windows that can drop down in case of rain. Capacity is 22 passengers and 21 passengers. Captains are US Coast Guard Certified. Both our Captain and mate were quite knowledgeable about local history, birds, plants, reptiles and more. Their keen eyes spot even small things, like a baby turtle sunning itself on a log.

We cruise by the town of Tavares. A long linear park anchors the city shoreline. Tavares has a certified seaplane airport. Small seaplanes are tied up along the shoreline. Plus, a replica of a three decker paddlewheel steamboat is tied up to a dock.

Our guide tells us there are a variety of seaplane tours including a bar hopping trip you can take where they fly you from one bar to the next. We cruise on, headed for an opening that signals the beginning of the Mount Dora canal.

The short canal, one and a quarter mile long, used to be the Elfin River, home to Timucuan Indians who were ousted by waves of settlers from Spain, France, and England. In the late 1800s the waterway was widened in part to accommodate steamboats and became known as the Dora Canal. It took 70 men two years to widen— endless digging.

Once done, three decker steamboats came up the Ocklawaha River and made their way across lakes and through Dora Canal all the way to Mount Dora. The steamboats brought passengers, freight, mail, all vital links to the outside world.

But then along came the railroads. In a bid to get rid of steamships, the railroad built a bridge across the Dora Canal, making it impossible for three decker steamships to pass. The steamships only made it to Mount Dora for three years.

At the start of the canal, both sides are heavily inhabited with small homes that have been there for a while. A sense of humor pervades. An entire village of gnome statues gathers at the water's edge on the right side. On the other side of the canal, more gnomes face the water. With a straight face our guide tells us the gnome village on the right is where a wedding is taking place. The gnome village on the left are the in-laws who were not invited.

We groan, or laugh, and move on. Both our captain and the mate take turns at the microphone, telling tall tales, bad jokes and pointing out wildlife along the way.

A lone anhinga sits on a tree limb drying its wings. Another X on the bingo cards for the word anhinga. These diving birds go deep looking for fish, then must dry their wings, weighted down with water. The males are all black, the females have rust brown throats. We see a male anhinga that has speared a small fish. It manages to turn the fish around and down it goes, headfirst. Impressive.

The houses fade into the background. We glide along, passing lots of cypress trees, mostly bare now as it is late fall. The mate is narrating, and he tells us about cypress knees, knobby things sticking up out of the water and mentions how slowly cypress trees grow. How slowly? An inch every ten years.

The pontoon boat turns around and heads back. Premier Boat Tours has their dock at the water's edge, just below the historic Lakeside Inn, founded in 1883.

Pulling up to the dock, the bingo card folks are pleased. Highest score, 24 different things spotted. And that reindeer? A Christmas light fixture in a reindeer shape at the dock. Bingo.

My boat tour

Date _____

_____

_____

_____

_____

Chapter 9

St. Johns River Nature Cruise

Duration: 2 hours

Cost: $35.68 adults. Call for all prices.

Location: Blue Spring State Park, 2100 W.

French Ave., Orange City, FL

Phone: 833-953-2583

Website:

https://bluespringadventures.com/tours/

Good to know: Park fills up quickly.

Wheelchair lift into the vessel. Mention

any accessibility needs when making a

reservation

Rainy gray day on the St. Johns River. It is late autumn, and we float along as if in a dream. Bare trees show their naked limbs. Leftover leaves wear fall colors, yellow and russet and bright red.

A leaf falls, whirling down like a spinning top, lands on the river surface and floats. It is a miniature message carrying whispers of colder days and chilly nights. Sweater weather.

I'm on the St. Johns River Nature Cruise, aboard a pontoon boat operated by Blue Spring Adventures. The boat tour leaves rain or shine. But if there is lighting within five miles, the trip can be cancelled. All that information is on the ticket. Reservations recommended.

While waiting to board, and walking on the boardwalk, one manatee was sighted in the springs but none as we cruise the river for two hours. That is the thing about nature cruises. What is seen on the tour depends on luck, time of day, and the season.

Alligators, our guide tells us, are seldom seen in the summer. Too hot for them, they like to hang out on the bottom of the river. But this is fall and late morning. Perhaps an alligator will emerge to sun itself on a log.

Yes! We see a baby alligator who hangs around long enough for lots of photos, then plunges in the river. Our guide has eagle eyes. She spots everything – vultures sitting high up in a tree, an anhinga drying its wings, a snapping turtle climbing up on a log, a bittern with its beak straight up, swaying with the grasses around it, a form of camouflage.

This is the manatee zone part of the river, so the boat cruises along at idle speed. Manatees favor Blue Springs State Park in winter, particularly January and February. When water gets cold in the Gulf of Mexico, up they come to the warm river waters. It is not uncommon to see manatees floating shoulder to shoulder in the shelter of Blue Springs.

Sitting near me is an extended family, three generations, from Scotland. They are both excited and charmed by everything seen on the tour. And I have taken my own advice. On this tour I sit in the first row up front. What a view!

Our guide points out a great blue heron nest high up in a tree. And she spots a troop of wild turkeys on the left side of the river, walking in a swampy area. This causes everyone on the boat to rush over to the left side for a look. Our lucky day. Wild turkeys. We won the wildlife lottery.

Maneuvering the boat close to the right side of the river, she shows us bald cypress trees and the knees growing up around them. They feel ancient, rooted in the river, aware of all the passing eons.

Long before railroads and interstate highways, rivers in Florida were the roads of choice. Ships came from Europe, docked at ports like Jacksonville, then goods transferred to tall steamboats – narrow in beam with shallow flat draft – perfect for rivers.

Sightseers came aboard along with would-be settlers and entrepreneurs seeking a future in citrus. The Florida tourist trade boomed with river trips. River steamboats were the only practical means of transportation. But by the 1880s many Florida cities were connected by railroads and the heyday of river steamboats ended.

Today's pontoon boats have the same narrow beam and shallow flat draft as the river steamboats. Pontoon boats have just one deck, usually covered, and just perfect for river tours, short cruises where you learn some Florida history, hopefully see lots of wildlife, and enjoy being guided on a floating adventure.

My boat tour

Date _____

_____

_____

_____

Chapter 10

DeLeon Springs Adventures Boat Tour

Duration: 50 minutes

Cost: $19 adults. All costs on website

Location: 601 Ponce de Leon Blvd., DeLeon Springs, FL, DeLeon Springs State Park

Phone: 855-980-2665

Website: https://deleonspringsadventures.com/tour/

Good to know: Park fees apply. Very popular destination. Arrive early

Inside DeLeon Springs State Park, 19 to 20 million gallons of water a day come out of DeLeon Springs and flow over a waterfall into Spring Garden Creek. Could this be the legendary Fountain of Youth? It certainly is a contender.

You will pass by this lovely waterfall while walking on your way to the booth for the DeLeon Springs Adventures Boat Tour.

This 50 minute boat tour starts on Spring Garden
Creek then floats into Spring Garden Lake and onto

Jones Island and a bit of Lake Woodruff National Wildlife Refuge. The waterways we are on today eventually run into the St. Johns River. That in turn, if we kept on going, runs from south to north, backwards, and empties into the Atlantic Ocean. All these rivers and tributaries were once wet highways a century ago. Steamboats with shallow draft plied these waters bringing goods, people, and tourists inland.

Having been on this boat tour several times, I'm immediately impressed once again with the lush landscape—trees of many kinds standing thick and deep on both sides of the river. Preservation of the natural landscape plays a part. Lake Woodruff NWR was established in 1964 as a migratory bird refuge, part of five million-plus acres purchased by US Fish & Wildlife Service with proceeds from the Federal Duck Stamp Program. Those trees have been around for a while. Migratory birds find them every year.

DeLeon Springs itself used to be a private attraction. The state purchased the springs and 55 acres for one million dollars. DeLeon Springs State Park became a reality. The Old Sugar Mill, known for having pancake griddles inserted into every table, and located near the waterfall, still serves breakfast and lunch. Swimming in the springs is immensely popular all year long.

Captain Kim points out something we can't see, but it is down there, underwater. Not far from the waterfall and the start of our tour, divers found a dugout canoe, some 5,000 to 6,000 years old. Native Americans were very familiar with this area.

A great blue heron stands still in the shallows, seemingly posing for photographs. The key word with seeing birds is "migratory." It is late spring now and many birds have, like the snowbirds they are, headed up north. They will be back in the fall. Captain Kim mentions the cormorants, they were here in large numbers but have migrated north.

A mullet jumps in front of the pontoon boat. It lands on the water with a slap. Captain Kim says the common theory is that mullet jump out of the water and slap the surface to get rid of parasites. But she suggests—perhaps they jump because it makes them happy.

We pass by big beds of spatterdock, also known as cow lily. This aquatic plant is like a buffet for wildlife.

Deer graze on it, while below water the rhizomes are eaten by beavers, muskrats, and nutria. Ducks and other waterfowl eat the seeds. The submerged portions provide habitats for large and small invertebrates. Spatterdock beds can be considered floating ecosystems.

Captain Kim notes that the water in places is just two feet deep. But she does not advise wading. Under the two feet sits at least six feet of muck, like decaying spatterdock.

Like most captains, she has an eagle eye for spotting wildlife. An alligator sunning itself near the spatterdock opens one eye as the boat approaches but he doesn't give up his sunny spot. Alligators and crocodiles need sunshine to thermoregulate, meaning they need outside sources of heat to warm their bodies. No sunscreen required.

Now we see a great egret. It still wears its mating plumage. This beautiful array of feathers almost caused their extinction. In the late nineteenth and early twentieth centuries more than 95% of great egrets in North America were killed for their plumes, which were used to decorate women's hats. The taking of plumes was banned around 1910. Great egret populations recovered.

For your tour consider bringing binoculars, a camera, sunglasses, and bug spray. You may need them all.

My boat tour

Date _____

_____

_____

_____

_____

Chapter 11

Loxahatchee Queen Pontoon Boat Tour

Duration: 90 minutes

Cost: $30 adults

Location: 16450 SE Federal Highway, Hobe Sound, FL

Phone: 772-546-2771

Website:https://www.floridastateparks.org/parks-and-trails/jonathan-dickinson-state-park

Good to know: Tour is tide dependent. Call ahead for times (561-746-1466). Park entrance fees apply

---

The Loxahatchee River is one of only two rivers in Florida designated as a national wild and scenic river. Where does the long name Loxahatchee come from? It is Seminole for river of turtles.

Boarding a midsize pontoon boat at a boat ramp inside Jonathan Dickinson State Park in Hobe Sound, the seats filled up fast. Half of them were occupied by middle schoolers, obviously on a field trip. They came complete with a teacher and several parents who looked a bit harried. The rest, like me, were visitors from many places. As we pulled away from the dock, I heard a student say, "There is no Wi-Fi here." Indeed.

Turtles didn't get the memo that they should be out in force for us as our pontoon boat maneuvered steadily down the river. There were three turtles sunning on a branch above the water. That was it.

The Loxahatchee twists and turns, with tributaries headed in all directions. Thick stands of red mangroves line each side of the river. So glad the captain knew where he was going. This trip has a destination—the Trapper Nelson Interpretive Site.

Called the Wild Man of the Loxahatchee, Vincent Natulkiewicz (or Nostokovich), born in 1909, also known as Vince "Trapper" Nelson, stood six feet four inches, and weighed 240 pounds. He settled here in the early 1930s. Over time he acquired 800 acres of land.

He made his living trapping, hunting, and fishing, then added a zoo, starting a business called "Trapper's Zoo and Jungle Garden." Nelson built docks, cages, cabins, and shelters, planted fruit trees, even added bamboo to the river's edge to make it look more jungle-like. A true off the grid entrepreneur.

Photographs show Nelson bare chested, wearing cutoffs, cowboy boots and a cowboy hat. He comes across larger than life. And stories back that up. One diner owner remembers him coming in, ordering pie, not just a piece but a whole pie, and eating it all right there.

Hundreds of visitors over the years managed to find Nelson and his site, learned about the river, saw its beauty and were surely a bit awed by Nelson himself.

With all the twists and turns to get there, and only possible on a high tide, how did he ever find this place so far from civilization? Find it he did. Stepping off the pontoon boat onto a dock, we immediately must climb uphill. Yes, uphill. In Florida if there is a two foot or more ascent above sea level, you are on high ground. Nelson, amazingly, found high ground. Buildings he built remain standing. Interpretive signs and photographs fill in his life story.

Gathering around several park rangers, the kids like Nelson immediately. A wild man. With murder in his history. He witnessed his stepbrother kill a man. Later Nelson testified against him, and the brother went to Raiford for 20 years. Disillusioned with city life, government, rules and regulations, Nelson retreated to the river. The rest is history—the trapping, the zoo, the gardens, the stories, including his reading of the Wall Street Journal regularly and investing in more and more land.

A health inspector, about the time Nelson was buying more land, declared his zoo unhygienic and demanded bathrooms be installed. They were, but the health department said they were "unsatisfactory." In 1960 he was forced to close his zoo. His income went away and his belief in conspiracy theories went up. He became a recuse and had a shotgun to discourage anyone from stepping on his land.

There is mystery about his death. He was found in 1968 on site, dressed in a suit, as if going to town. He died from a shotgun blast to his stomach, later ruled a suicide. Trapper's family sold all his land to a developer. In a land swap, the Florida Park Service acquired Trapper Nelson Interpretive site and maintains it.

Wandering the grounds with the park rangers, the tour group comes upon a car in almost pristine condition. Turns out there is a back door, so to speak, to Nelson's land. A private road, so private, anyone using it needs permission for access. That road is how the park rangers get to work every day.

The boat tour passengers, however, need to leave, like now, as the tide is turning and if it gets too low, well, we'd be spending the night at the site. At that prospect, passengers get aboard the boat rather quickly, a park ranger casts off the line, and the pontoon boat floats leisurely back to the park dock.

Blue skies are dotted with puffy white clouds. The river is serene, peaceful. Gliding past kayaks, an anhinga drying its wings, and those turtles sunning themselves, it is easy to imagine this place as an Eden in South Florida.

My boat tour

Date

Chapter 12

Sea Life Safari

Duration: 90 minutes

Cost: $27.95 ages 3 and up varies by date

Location: Clearwater Marine Aquarium,

249 Windward Passage, Clearwater, FL

Phone: 727-441-1790

Website: https://www.cmaquarium.org

Good to know: Not wheelchair accessible

Motes of light glitter on the surface of Clearwater Bay. I'm floating along on a large, covered pontoon boat called Sea Life Safari. This is an eco-boat tour that cast off from a dock at Clearwater Marine Aquarium.

Right now, I feel suspended in time and place, caught between a slab of cerulean, blue sky besotted by billowing white clouds and a surface of turquoise colored water that hides another world, an aquatic world, swimming in the depths.

Described as a 90-minute experience in citizen science, the Sea Life Safari quickly gets down to business. Our captain guides the boat away from the dock to the center of the estuary and cuts the engine. Two crew members prepare a large net and throw it overboard. After starting the engine and a short time dragging the net, the crew brings the net aboard and begins removing sea life that got tangled in the net.

Those of us in the back of the pontoon boat can't really see what is happening up front where the net was lowered. Lesson learned for next time: pick a seat up front.

As the net is pulled up, I can't help but wonder if the captured sea life feels this is all deja vu: "Oh no, here we go again, another day, another haul." At least the crew puts everything back towards the end of the tour, albeit in a different part of the bay.

Later crew members make the rounds with sea life in containers. Everyone gets a good look. One catch: a small slender fish, about one inch long, white with black eyes. The crew could not identify it. Photographs were taken and a crew member will do the research later for a name.

Next stop: a desert island. Not quite deserted. There is one tree. This is a small shell island. Those that want to walk around depart the boat on a ramp, taking off our shoes and getting our feet wet. Shelling. The name of the

game. Lots of shells!

A crew member walks the shoreline looking closely at the water. She returns with a starfish, a good find and quite popular with those taking photos. Everyone eventually back on board and accounted for, the ramp is raised.

Our boat cruises slowly across the bay heading back to the aquarium dock. A dolphin makes an appearance. Brown pelicans fly overhead. Ah, life observed above and below the water. How wonderful it is to glide along, be a spectator, free of having to be in charge, someone else at the helm, all earthly cares like heavy traffic and to do lists left behind for a short, memorable time on the water.

Crew members begin emptying out the sea life containers back into the bay. A crew member tries to put the starfish back into the water, but the starfish clings firmly, all six legs, to the container. One by one she pries its legs loose. It takes a while, but the starfish finally gets unattached from the container and returned to its native environment. Passengers cheer.

Back at the dock, off go the passengers, who exit through the aquarium. Some of us have shells in our pockets to add to our collections back home.

A few observations: although this is a covered pontoon boat, I recommend hat and sunglasses and sun protection. There will be time on the island, all wide open to the elements.

When on board, a narrator speaks into a microphone. But if the captain pushes the engine to get from Point A to Point B, the sound of the speaker is completely drowned out by engine noise.

Naturally all that citizen science can be considered hard work. The reward is lunch. I head for Frenchy's Rockaway Grill on Clearwater Beach. My menu: she crab soup and their famous grouper sandwich.

To cap off the day, Pier 60 is rightly famous as a sunset event destination. From 5 p.m. to 9 p.m. mingle with artisans and street performers plus celebrate the often glorious sunset over the Gulf of Mexico.

My boat tour

Date _____

_____

_____

_____

_____

Chapter 13

St. Nicholas Boat Line Sponge

Diving Exhibition

Duration: 40 minutes

Cost: $18 adults. Call for all prices.

Location: 693 Dodecanese Blvd., Tarpon

Springs, FL

Phone: 727-942-6425

Website:https://www.stnicholasboatline.com

Good to know: Not handicapped accessible.

Hours vary. They try to be closed on

Sundays. Call ahead

The St. Nicholas VII gleams with fresh paint—white on the sides, blue and orange railings, and posts. This is a true working Greek sponge boat, vintage, hewed by hand and no longer being built. Passengers are literally stepping aboard living history.

"We've been doing this for 100 years," says George, Greek boat captain and owner of St. Nicholas Boat Line in Tarpon Springs. Sponging is a family way of life. In 1924 Captain Michael J. Billiris started this boat line. It continues to be operated by the same family.

Casting off, the St. Nicholas VII starts a forty minute round trip cruise along the historic Sponge Docks of Tarpon Springs on the Anclote River. The docks are still dedicated today to commercial fishing boats and sponge boats.

As we float along George tells us that the diving suit was invented in 1837. Before that hooking was the method used to get sponges. A crew member had a box with a piece of glass in the bottom. In shallow water, thirty feet or less, the glass box was lowered, and the boat floated along. If a sponge was spotted it was hooked using a long pole.

When the diving suit made its debut, everything changed. With a heavily weighted diving suit and air delivered through an air hose, a diver could walk on the bottom, hook sponges, put them in a bag and send the bag up to the surface.

Credit for starting the Tarpon Springs sponge industry goes to John Cheyney and John Cocoris. Cheyney launched his first boat in 1890, using hooking as the technique for getting sponges. That same year he opened the Anclote River and Rock Island Sponge Company.

Then came divers, walking on the bottom, and they found some of the best sponge beds in deeper water. In fact, better sponges come from deeper water. More divers were needed. And they came. In 1905 more than 500 Greek men arrived in Tarpon Springs!

The heyday of the diving suit used for sponging lasted from 1905 to 1930. Boats were built. Notice the VII in the name of our tour boat today, this boat is the seventh one for the St. Nicholas line, built here in Tarpon Springs.

Sponging during that time produced eighty percent of the world's sponges. Small boats stayed out two to three weeks and large boats from two to three months. Sponge boats traveled from ten to 100 miles out into the Gulf of Mexico all the way from Apalachicola to Key West. Divers worked from thirty feet down to two hundred feet. George introduces Demetri, a crew member and former diver who dove to a depth of two hundred feet. Passengers clap in admiration. That is quite a feat.

Sponges are a primitive sedentary aquatic invertebrate with a soft, porous body that is typically supported by a framework of fibers or calcareous or glassy spicules. Sponges draw in a current of water to extract nutrients and oxygen. This is a renewable resource. Divers are now required to use a knife and leave a half an inch at the base of a sponge so it will grow again.

George has a basket full of different kinds of sponges. Time for show and tell. He holds up a large sponge called a wool sponge. It is the most absorbent and most popular sponge. A wool sponge can be used for washing cars, in the bath, around the house. It will last several years. Just squeeze it dry after use. The sponge gets passed from passenger to passenger.

The second most popular is the yellow sponge and so it goes through five different kinds of sponges. It is quite a process to clean a sponge. George says he'll save that story for later. Sponging goes on year round. There is no limit, no season. All focus turns from sponges to the diver, a young Greek eighteen years old.

He is also named George, and this is just his second month on the job. Naturally he is related, a second cousin.

Wearing a diving suit made of two layers of canvas, more is added, weighted shoes, a big breast plate, a huge helmet made of copper. By the time he is fully dressed there is 172 pounds of weight.

Photo opportunities abound – when the diver is dressed, coming back on the boat from being overboard in the water. And it is not just the children who get excited. Adults happily line up to have their pictures taken with the diver. A dog that came with a couple struck a pose with the diver.

The boat stops near the shore. The diver, now fully suited, sits on the railing with feet dangling overboard then, on a signal, he is pushed overboard. Everyone goes to that side, watching the trail of bubbles under the surface. It is not long before he comes to the surface with a live sponge. Back on board, the live sponge is passed around.

Turning the boat around, George points out the bags of sponges on boats at the docks. Those are completely dried sponges. Processing sponges includes stacking sponges, covering them with a tarp, rotating the sponges every two to three days. Gradually animal matter dries up. Anything that helps this process is done, such as stepping on sponges, and squeezing them dry. Eventually they end up in net bags, all dry, clean, ready to sell.

Bidders come on auction days. Sponges are laid out on the docks by different kinds and sizes. It is a silent bid process. A buyer will put a bid on a piece of paper. They will be buying the whole lot. These bidders represent hardware stores, home improvement stores, all kinds of places that use real sponges. FYI, sponges cannot be sold to the public off the boat. Buy at Sponge Dock shops.

My boat tour

Date _____

_____

_____

_____

_____

Chapter 14

Tampa History Cruise

Duration: 90 minutes

Cost: $30.77 adults

Location: Behind the Tampa Bay History
Center, 801 Old Water Street, Tampa, FL

Phone: 813-900-3288

Website:
https://www.tampawatertaxico.com

Good to know: Not handicapped accessible

Long ago and not so far away Florida's first peoples
inhabited this peninsula some 10,000 years ago.
European explorers arrived in the 1500s. Today this port
city has up to three cruise ships arriving every day. It is
also the industrial capital of West Central Florida.

Where am I? Tampa. Standing in line at water taxi
dock #3 located behind the Tampa Bay History Center in
the Water Street neighborhood. Time to board the blue
boat with the yellow top for an hour and a half cruise on

the Hillsborough River. This history cruise is operated by the Tampa Water Taxi Company.

Showing our tickets purchased online we step aboard a converted Navy PT boat, open air seating. Richard is our guide. He is clearly enthusiastic about Tampa's history and the ongoing transformation of a waterfront into a bustling port plus vibrant neighborhoods worth visiting.

First, we glide past the industrial waterfront area. Large fuel tanks are embellished with murals. There are berths for cruise ships. When cruise ships arrive, passengers are disgorged at 8 am to roam around Tampa then picked up at 4 p.m.

Moored at a dock is a fully restored piece of maritime history—an American Victory Ship built in 45 days during World War II. Now a museum, this is one of only four operational WWII ships in the United States. It is a beauty.

Richard has more to say but it is hard to hear him over the roar of diesel engines. He lowers the engines to half speed. It is much easier to hear his stories.

We cruise by a waterfront neighborhood full of mega mansions. Richard tells us the biggest one has a swimming pool inside the house and the square footage is the same as a Target store, about 125,000 square feet.

Now we're floated alongside the Tampa Riverwalk, a 2.6 mile open space and pedestrian walkway that has parks, sculptures plus access to shopping and restaurants. As we glide along, we see families, joggers, dog walkers

on the riverwalk. Looks inviting, a very good reason to come back another time and walk the walk.

On the other side of the river is the Henry B. Plant Museum housed in the south wing of Plant Hall on the University of Tampa's campus. Easy to recognize the campus by the minarets—a photo op.

Naturally, because this is Tampa, we pass a fully rigged pirate ship, moored quietly now. But it will be full of pirates during the next Gasparilla Invasion and Parade, an annual event held in January on the fourth Saturday. Richard relates that the waterways are so full of boats for the Gasparilla Invasion that you can literally walk from one side of the river to the other by jumping from boat to boat.

Downtown office buildings rise high above the waterline. One building has multiple corners. That was deliberate—more corner offices to sell. Richard pointed out this oddity to us. I would have missed it completely otherwise.

Seeing Tampa's many different areas from the water certainly inspired a desire to sample places like the

Waterworks Park in historic Tampa Heights, newly built up complete with an outdoor concert area.

We return to the dock and amble off on our separate ways. Paid parking is available at nearby lots. Build in time to arrive early and deal with parking. The day of my tour the pay station was closed. A suggested parking app had to be downloaded. Time duration for parking? Add a couple of hours. Perhaps have lunch at the Columbia Café inside the Tampa Bay History Center and explore the Center. Or stroll one block over to an entire veranda area filled with food trucks.

My boat tour

Date _____

_____

_____

_____

Chapter 15

> ## Sea Life Encounter Eco Tour
>
> Duration: 2 hours
>
> Cost: $36 adult. All costs on website
>
> Location: 1600 Ken Thompson Pkwy, City Island, Sarasota, FL
>
> Phone: 941-388-4200
>
> Website: https://www.sarasotabayexplorers.com
>
> Good to know: Arrive 30 minutes ahead of tour Boat leaves on time. No refunds if you are late

Remember science class? Well, that class is back in a fun way. Three times a day the Sarasota Bay Explorers launches a sea life encounter eco tour for all ages. Join a marine biologist for a marine life and nature tour of Sarasota and Roberts Bay, including observation and hands-on exploration of sea life specimens.

Our covered pontoon boat, full of passengers, leaves Mote Marine at 11 am for the first tour of the day. The

sun is shining, the sky is blue with bright white cumulus clouds. There is no wind. Perfect weather for being afloat. Sky, our guide, asks questions. How deep is Sarasota Bay? Hands go up. Answers vary from six feet to forty feet. She accepts them all then gives the correct answer.

Turns out the average depth of Sarasota Bay is six to ten feet. Who knew it was so shallow? Not me. Sky, a New Collage graduate, points out the different colors of the water's surface – darker where there are seagrass beds, lighter in the shallower areas.

Sky shares lively stories about the ecology, history, and folklore of Sarasota. In the center of the boat is a table with a small aquarium and an assortment of containers with sea water. Already there are a few specimens, like a sea urchin and some mollusks. More will be added after a trawl in Sarasota Bay.

The pontoon boat passes under the John Ringling Bridge. Everyone looks up. Quite a different perspective than the usual driving on the bridge.

Sarasota Bay is home to some 170 dolphins. They are extensively studied and have been for decades. Markings on dorsal fins identify them. Cell phones start clicking when the first dolphin is spotted. This one has no dorsal fin markings. Sky tells us if we see two coming up to the surface at the same time, they are probably a mother and her calf.

Five white pelicans float nearby. They are winter visitors. A brown pelican flies overhead. Soon a brown pelican and white pelican floating together are spotted, with the white pelican being the much larger bird. More photos.

106

The bay was dredged years ago to make a channel more suitable for navigation. The dredged material became the stuff of spoil islands. Sarasota and Roberts Bay are dotted with spoil islands.

Keeping a respectful distance, the pontoon boat, now in Roberts Bay, idles near a large rookery. The island is thick with red mangroves and these trees are packed with great blue herons, roseate spoonbills, and other wading birds, all making nests, tending young and keeping a sharp eye out for predators.

Speaking of predators, the reason this island in the middle of the bay stays so crowded is that the birds know not to nest on spoil islands close to shore. Predators like snakes, feral cats, racoons, foxes, Sky says, can wade or swim from the mainland to a close spoil island and do their damage.

Two roseate spoonbills take flight from the rookery. There is a collective gasp aboard the boat. It is quite a sight, bright pink wings flapping, very photogenic! Their red coloring comes from their diet, an organic pigment called carotenoid produced by plants, algae, bacteria, and fungi. The same carotenoid gives bright pink coloring to flamingos.

One hour into a two-hour tour, it is time to stretch our legs. The boat nudges the sand at Big Edwards, a spoil island in Roberts Bay. Down goes a ramp. A volunteer gathers everyone on the beach to hear about invasive Australian pines, like the ones growing all over this island.

Big and Little Edwards Islands are both designated as parks. Both large islands are popular destinations for boaters seeking a quiet, shady island for a picnic.

Our pontoon boat casts off and the trawl of the bay begins. Up comes lots of sea grasses. Both Sky and a volunteer carefully sift through the grasses, looking for specimens. Fish go into the tank. Small things, like a starfish, go into the containers. These are passed around for all to see. A large welk gets the touch test by passengers. So does the sea urchin. But no enthusiasm for touching the spider crab, who is not pleased to be aboard. Most sea life gets returned to the bay. Some stay round for the next tour.

And the boat returns to the dock. Science class is over. Delightful, and a fine day to be out on the bay.

My boat tour

Date _____

South Florida

Chapter 16

Naples Sightseeing Day Cruise

Duration: 90 minutes

Cost: Adults $46

Location: 1146 6th Ave. South, Naples, FL

Phone: 239-263-4949

Website: https://www.purefl.com

Good to know: Free parking. Arrive no later than 30 minutes before departure time. No outside drinks or food

Double Sunshine. That is the name for a double-decker sightseeing boat docked at Tin City in Naples. What a great name! This ocean-capable boat can hold up to 149 passengers on the two decks. Onboard is a small bar with drinks and food for sale and bathrooms are available.

At the entrance to Tin City there is a Pure Florida ticket booth for buying tour tickets or, if you paid online and have the printout of your email, just head for the dock behind Tin City. Benches in a tiki hut at the end of the dock provide a shady place to sit. Boarding begins fifteen minutes before departure time.

There are three steps up to boarding the boat plus a handrail on both sides of the steps. Tempting to say this vessel is not handicapped accessible but the day of my trip a woman in a wheelchair arrived. She stood up, used the handrails, climbed the three stairs, and then the wheelchair was folded up and taken aboard. So, accessibility is negotiable.

Captain Josh warns passengers there will be four loud blasts as we get ready to cast off. Yep. Four blasts. Then a bit of a boat traffic jam on the Gordon River. The Double Sunshine is backing up and moving away from the dock. Also in the river a pontoon boat traveling upstream and a small vessel coming downstream. Much too crowded. Someone had to give way. The first mates on Double Sunshine call out to the two boats trying to find a solution.

The pontoon boat comes to a stop. The smaller boat finally backs up and the large Double Sunshine has room to maneuver. As we idle along, leaving those two boats behind us, Captain Josh asks passengers to look at the water. It is tea brown, not pollution, but tannic acid.

We float past marinas where small to medium sized boats are all on lifts, out of the water, meaning less algae on the bottoms and less staining from tannic acid. Next are marinas for bigger boats. Every slip is taken. Mega yachts hug the prime spots at the end of marina docks.

Naples is located on the Gulf of Mexico. Water traffic is constant and varied, from a dinghy to catamarans, pontoon boats, trawlers, stone crab boats, bass boats, flats boats, cabin cruisers, sailboats. Not only are the marinas full, but every stately waterfront mansion has a boat dock and a boat or two tied up or on lifts.

Cruising along in Naples Bay. Captain Josh points out the Naples Yacht Club. To get in, he tells us, requires three recommendations, being a property owner in Naples, interviews and an application fee of $40,000 for consideration of membership. Even if you pass all that with flying colors, it could be three to five years before a spot opens. Meanwhile, an annual fee of $40,000 is due.

On our starboard (right) side is Aqualane Shores, built in the 1940s, using dredge and fill to create deep water channels. In those days, a lot in Aqualane Shores cost $6,000 and a house could be built for the same amount.

Next door to Aqualane Shores is the Port Royal development. In the late 1940s John Sample, a pioneer in radio advertising from Chicago, bought two square miles of marshland at the southern tip of Naples. Bound by the Gulf of Mexico on the west side and Naples Bay on the east, a few years of dredge and fill created 600 real estate lots with access to Gordon pass. A lot cost $12,000 and a house could be built for the same amount.

Sample, we are told, didn't care for musicians, actors, athletes, even politicians. He preferred selling to people that had great wealth, what he called "quiet wealth" like CEOs.

The wealth may be quiet, but its display is grand. One home has connecting parts, one building attached to another, some 45,000 square feet. Employees working there have their own place to live, right on the grounds. For a long time, Sample refused to allow homes with a second story. That may explain why the houses spread out horizontally.

And yet we see few people about as we motor past all this history and wealth. Many houses have hurricane shutters up, no cushions on deck chairs outside, no one swimming laps in the pools. Captain Josh says eighty-eight percent of the homes in Port Royal are occupied from two to five weeks a year.

A young manatee surfaces on the starboard side of the Double Sunshine, causing quite a stir among the passengers. Pelicans fly by. Anhingas dry their wings on pilings. Wildlife, it seems, is oblivious to the wealth displayed by acres of waterfront homes. Passing yet another large home, a long series of connected buildings all painted pink, we learn it is for sale. Price: $295 million. Currently it is the highest price for a house in Naples.

The Double Sunshine goes through Gordon Pass and into the Gulf of Mexico. Here the waters are a deep sea green with sparkles of sunlight scattered like jewels on the surface. Should the boat continue straight on across the Gulf of Mexico, Captain Josh tells us, we'd end up in Texas. But not today.

We turn around and head back to Naples Bay. Soon two dolphins join us, riding our wake. They leap out of the water, then keep pace with us almost all the way back to the dock. Quite exciting. Of course, cell phones are set to video. Everyone hoping to record a leaping moment.

Just so you know, Pure Florida has a spreadsheet full of cruises—sightseeing, shelling, dolphin watching, sunset cruises, every day of the week, all day long.

Their motto: Seas the day.

My boat tour

Date _____

_____

_____

_____

_____

Chapter 17

Everglades National Park Adventures, Ten
Thousand Island Boat Tour

Duration: 2 hours

Cost: from $48

Location: 929 Dupont St., Everglades City, FL

Phone: 239-330-1902

Website: https://www.evergladesnationalpark
adventures.com

Good to know: handicapped accessible

Everglades City thrives on tourism. Positioned on the Barron River and Chokoloskee Bay, this city is a gateway to Everglades National Park and Ten Thousand Islands. Water tours and fishing tours are popular.

While we waited to board a pontoon boat for a Ten Thousand Island tour, we see four air boats, their passengers wearing ear protectors, rumble past, heading for the open waters of Everglades National Park.

Then the ramp was set in place for us to board the boat. It is an easy, flat ramp, totally accessible. Fifty-two people of all ages find seats. The horn hoots. Our adventure begins.

As we slowly motor down the river, Captain Dawain points out the sights and gives a bit of history. He is a native, attended the K-12 school in Everglades City. There were eight people in his graduating class. The school is still there. He tells us it is the last K-12 school in Florida.

An advertising entrepreneur named Barron Gift Collier arrived in the 1920s, bought big chunks of land and lots of buildings, including an existing structure he expanded into a hotel and named the Rod and Gun Club. It became a hub for his wealthy friends who came to visit and fish. They especially liked to shoot tarpon with spear guns.

Still standing today with a restaurant inside, and cottages on the grounds for rent, our pontoon boat floats by this living piece of history. Note: if you want to visit the Rod and Gun Club restaurant later, be advised they only accept cash, no credit cards.

Collier had roads built, including Broadway Avenue, which became the main drag. A train depot and trolly were located here. Also built a hospital and he even built homes for workers. Much of this history can be found in the Museum of the Everglades, located in a historic building on Broadway Avenue.

The 1928 Okeechobee hurricane wiped out the local cattle industry. Collier bought the former cattle land and built a nine-hole golf course. Years later a landing strip was installed. Pilots learning to fly still use it for touch and go practice.

Already birds are being sighted. An osprey building a nest. Purple martin houses awaiting the annual arrival of purple martins. A group of pelicans flying in V formation go over our boat, headed for Ten Thousand Islands and open water.

Captain Dawain points out a royal tern sitting on a channel marker. "You can always tell which way the wind is blowing," he says, "because royal terns always face into the wind."

The pontoon boat glides out of the river and into the open water of Chokoloskee Bay. All around us and off in the distance, are islands, low shell strips dotted with mangroves. There are also Calusa Indian mounds.

Generations ago, the Spaniards brought European diseases that decimated the local Indian population. Driven away, the Calusa became part of the Seminole Indians, living deep in the Everglades. This is the only Indian tribe to have never signed a peace treaty with the United States.

Captain Dawain invites questions from passengers. One young girl keeps raising her hand. She asks good questions. Her family nods their heads. Yep. This is the inquisitive one. The rest of the passengers, me included, look forward to hearing her next question.

We pass a marker that is the official boundary line for Everglades National Park. One must wonder, are there really ten thousand islands and if so, who counted them all?

Dolphin fins appear right alongside the boat. There is a rush of people to that side, looking for a sighting. One species new to the area and sometimes sighted are flamingos, blown here by storms. Captain Dawain notes two flamingos were sighted on an island. We are prepared for pink, but it was not to be on our trip.

Coming close to an island where bald eagles have a nest, the pontoon boat edges in close enough to see the nest, but the parents are not around. Captain Dwayne tells us fledgling eagles can stay around the nest for up to two years.

Turning around to head back to the dock, more dolphins appear. Cameras click. Video whirls.

While the First Mate pilots the boat, Captain Dawain walks around the boat to take pictures with people's phones of groups, families, individuals. Fun!

My boat tour

Date _____

_____

_____

_____

_____

Chapter 18

Jungle Queen Riverboat Cruise, Fort Lauderdale

Duration: 90 minutes

Cost: $31.50 adults ages 13 and up

Location: 801 Seabreeze Avenue,

Fort Lauderdale, Fl

Phone: 954-462-5596

Website: https://www.junglequeen.com

Good to know: two tours a day, 12 noon & 2:30 pm

The Jungle Queen Riverboat Cruise is Fort Lauderdale's longest running tourist attraction. There is something comforting about boarding a boat that has history. Their riverboats of various sizes and shapes have been floating along the waterways of Fort Lauderdale since 1935. The third generation of the same family operates the business today. With that kind of resume, you know from the get-go this boat tour will be fun.

The Jungle Queen Riverboat is in the same complex as the Bahia Yachting Center on A1A. Mega yachts, easily in the three million dollar class and beyond, are tied to the docks.

There is paid parking, $5 an hour. Usually, spaces are all gone in the front near the street but are much more available behind the center. The Jungle Queen has a voucher that saves some money on parking. You get it while onboard and scan it in when departing the center.

A sandwich board on the riverboat dock welcomes passengers in three languages—English, Spanish and French. A photographer will take your photo, pick it up later in the cruise. Early boarders like me head upstairs and take seats for top level viewing. Everyone is laughing and talking, and we haven't even left the dock yet.

The Jungle Queen is a two story replica of a real riverboat. Their bottom deck is handicapped accessible. There is a flight of stairs to climb to the upper deck. Alcoholic and nonalcoholic beverages available for sale at the bar. No hats needed on this trip. All seats undercover. Deck chairs have a stencil of the riverboat embedded in the back, an elegant touch.

Departing at 12 noon sharp, as advertised, Arlene takes the microphone. She is our host and commentator for the trip. Arlene advises us to look to the left to see the tallest diving platform in the Western Hemisphere. We look. It is part of the International Swimming Hall of

Fame. Used to be the tallest diving platform in the world but a taller one now exists in Asia.

The New River is not actually a river but a tidal estuary, a channel with many tributaries and it connects to the Everglades. It is also narrow. We glide along easily looking up close and personal into the gardens and backs of glorious Mediterranean revival houses. These grand edifices were built in an era when excess and exquisite beauty came together in structures that still stand tall today.

In the 1890s Mary Brickell and her husband William bought large tracts of land in Fort Lauderdale, much of it on the waterfront. That property was sold, and waterfront homes built. Arlene points to the right, telling us that house was designed in the shape of a butterfly. With a bit of a squint, we see it —especially when she points out two spiral staircases coming down from the second floor to the ground floor. These represent the antennae. Amazing.

There is no side yard for this home. So where is the garage? Turns out the first floor is a ten-car garage. Ah, you can only learn this kind of fun fact on a river tour! This home sold for $22 million in the spring of 2022. For obvious reasons, the area we are floating by is called Millionaire's Row.

Johnny Weissmuller, Olympic swimmer, and Tarzan of movie fame owned a home on this row. Naturally it had a swimming pool and diving board. He practiced his Tarzan yell then dived into the pool.

The first mega mansion here was built for Gloria Vanderbilt. There is another mansion built Harry Potter style. It is easy to get caught up in the rich and famous storyline. Arlene points out that while there is plenty of "long money" some of the richest people on the waterfront were ordinary people, like you and me, not born with a silver spoon, who had an idea and made it happen.

"If you have an idea how to make life easier, sell it," she advises.

Like Wayne Huizenga, who started a hauling business that turned into Waste Management. He did the same with Auto Nation, starting with a few dealerships, also Blockbuster Video. Oh, and then there was the sports stadium. All from humble beginnings.

She asks where we are from—all over the map. New York, Ukraine, St. Louis, Michigan, New Zealand. Arlene encourages getting the photos. "You are making history," she says. Turns out people arrive years after having their photo taken, bringing it with them, to celebrate an anniversary or birthday.

At one point we stop close to shore. The reason: a tugboat is towing a mega yacht up the river and must pass. Mega yacht owners are not allowed to steer their own boats. They must hire a captain and crew. And then, on the narrow New River, even the captain can't steer, due to concerns about collisions with waterfront property. Hence the tugboats.

Moving on, we float by the old yellow Riverside Hotel, built in 1936 on Las Olas Blvd. It was the first hotel in Fort Lauderdale. Ronald Reagan did the ribbon cutting. And she points out Riverwalk Fort Lauderdale, considered to be "Florida's most beautiful mile."

We float under the Andrews Avenue bridge, an old bridge that opens on demand. She points out restaurants and parks, places to visit once back on land. Then on to the cruise ship area, a turnaround for going back to the Jungle Queen dock.

The cityscape skyline for Fort Lauderdale has some high rises but not many. Arlene tells of a mayor who tried and succeeded in finally getting the height restrictions lifted. So, the skyline is changing. Arlene advises that in five to ten years the Fort Lauderdale skyline will look like Miami.

My boat tour

Date _____

Chapter 19

> ### Island Queen Millionaires Row Cruise
>
> Duration: 90 minutes
>
> Cost: $35 adults
>
> Location: Bayside Marketplace – 401 Biscayne Blvd, Miami, FL
>
> Phone: 844-664-1063
>
> Website: https://islandqueencruises.com
>
> Good to know: Buy ticket online, exchange for voucher at ticket booth inside Bayside Marketplace

For someone who lives in a midsize Florida city, like me, arriving in Miami means going from midsize to metropolis in a heartbeat. A shock. Like moving from a slow waltz to disco madness. Miami throbs with a population of almost 450,000 and is in Miami-Dade County housing 2.7 million people. Those numbers alone raise the decibel level.

Arriving at Bayside Marketplace, a huge waterfront venue with a sprawling mall and hotels, music blared out of every storefront in the marketplace. Walkways were crowded. Age range was mostly people in their 30s to 50s. Family groups. Tourists with guidebooks. Friends in big clusters. Hawkers galore, shouting, waving brochures and menus, vying for your attention outside boat tours and restaurants. People talking loudly in multiple languages, mostly English and Spanish.

I even had to lean into the ticket counter to speak to the Island Queen boat person, there was so much surrounding noise. If you buy a ticket online you must exchange that email confirmation for a voucher 45 minutes ahead of departure. Pressure to be ahead of departure time!

Finding the ticket booth took effort. When buying a ticket online, the recommendation is to watch a YouTube video of how to find the ticket booth in the marketplace. The fact that you are advised watch a YouTube video on getting to the booth should have been a clue it wasn't going to be easy.

I watched it. Only limited help. There is also a video on ADA compliance. I didn't find this to be true. The ticket counter person pointed out a flight of stairs going down to the dock. Once aboard the boat there is a flight of stairs up to the second level.

You should know the Island Queen departs from directly behind the ticket booth. But on the walkway, there is no sign that says this. The ticket booth person advises walking down the walkway to the next booth, a booth for a different boat, and there would be the stairs down to the dock. It is not until you are down on the dock that there are Island Queen signs.

The line formed on the dock for boarding 15 minutes before departure time. While waiting to board, a photographer will take your photo with friends, and you can hold an Island Queen life preserver. Prints are made while we float along and then the photographer offers them for sale.

Departure was scheduled for 1 p.m. People were still boarding at 1:15 p.m. We finally cast off for the 90 minute tour in Biscayne Bay and immediately get quite a good panoramic view of downtown Miami skyscrapers.

Topside open seating is the place to be for best views. It is also the location for the bar. The lower level is café style with round tables and chairs.

Pablo, the narrator, gives a short talk in English about where the life jackets are located, then repeats the same talk in Spanish. That will be the narration form, English and Spanish, for the trip.

This millionaire boat tour is aptly named. He points off to the right. There sit two mega yachts, longer than the docks they are tied to. Three million dollars, that is what just one of them costs.

Advising us to look to the left, there is a high rise apartment building, one of many. We learn an apartment is for sale in that building, 3.5 million dollars for a 3 bedroom, 3 bath apartment. Some currently famous people, whose names go right over my head, also live there.

Floating along, Pablo points out old apartment structures where Columbian drug lord Pablo Escobar once rented apartments. Plus, a house he built was demolished in 2016 and allegedly cocaine and money were found under four feet of concrete.

A series of islands on the left side of the boat are connected by bridges. All have mega homes. It seems every square inch has a structure. Old Mediterranean homes are torn down, replaced by glass edifices built by the rich and currently famous. Prices, we are told, range from $3 to $15 million.

As we go past Star Island, Pablo even points out an empty lot (not really, it has grass and trees) and tells us a developer owns this. That would be Stuart Miller, CEO of the giant development company Lennar.

Miller recently sold a spec mansion on Star Island for $49.5 million. The story is an historic structure sat on the property. Since he could not tear it down Miller had it moved to one end of the property and then built the large glass spec house where the historic home once stood. Our narrator casually notes Miller is single. He lets everyone know this in English and Spanish.

We cruise by Fisher Island, a private 226-acre island only accessible by ferry, helicopter, or boat. A ferry is departing as we go by. That ferry service runs 24 hours a day. High rise condos, homes, and a golf course are visible. A quick look later at real estate for sale on the island shows home prices from $38 to $42 million. Does that include ferry service?

Our double decker pontoon boat looks positively puny as we float by PortMiami and a huge container ship tied up to a dock. Immense cranes are nearby along with cruise ship docking. Billed as the cruise capital of the world, the port debarked over 7 million passengers in 2023. A total of 23 cruise lines currently dock at PortMiami.

We return on time to Bayside Marketplace. Curiously, we exit a much shorter way, to the left, than when we entered. Perhaps that long dock line for boarding was set up for the photographer to do his thing.

My boat tour

Date _____

_____

_____

_____

_____

Chapter 20

> Key Largo Princess Glass Bottom Boat
>
> Duration: 2 hours
>
> Cost: Ages 12 and up $55
>
> Location: 99701 Overseas Hwy, Key Largo, FL
>
> Phone: 305-451-4655
>
> Website: https://keylargoprincess.com
>
> Good to know: Check-in under the name you gave when making the reservation have ID available if asked
>
> Lower level is handicapped accessible, second level is not

A 75-foot, double decker large motor yacht named the Key Largo Princess shares dock space with the African Queen, a very small steam driven boat. Yes, that African Queen, the real deal, from the movie of the same name! Restored and tied up at the Holiday Inn docks in Key Largo.

The Princess, a glass bottomed boat, leaves the dock three times a day for excursions offshore to view live coral reefs at John Pennekamp Coral Reef State Park and Key Largo National Marine Sanctuary.

The lower level of the Princess is handicapped accessible, enclosed and is air conditioned. While standing in line, waiting to board, a crew member strongly advises passengers to forego downstairs and climb the stairs to the second level for the 45-minute ride out and back to the reef. He suggests the open air will help reduce the chance of seasickness.

Our trip fortunately features blue skies, puffy white clouds and no wind. That means very little rock and roll out on the ocean. When the boarding ramp is opened, we all opt to climb the steep stairs up to the second level. Seating is minimal. Most choose to stand. The benches for seating are not undercover. Hat and sunglasses, and sunscreen, recommended.

Soon after leaving the dock, the bar opens on the second level for drinks and snacks. Good to know as outside food and drinks are not allowed.

We idle pass condominiums and vacation homes, then out into the ocean, full throttle ahead. Finally, we are there, and everyone goes downstairs. The large viewing windows are set flat so there is no distortion of what we see under the water. What an amazing sight! We all lean over the railing, looking through the glass bottom. The water is sea green, a bright green color like new leaves on trees in the spring, and the ocean floor is alive with hard coral, in many shapes from gray brain coral to brown waving fronds of staghorn and elkhorn corals. Schools of small fish move in fast spurts, weaving around the coral reefs.

We have Nemo and Dory moments, seeing clown fish and banner fish and blue tang. Passengers are invited to sit with feet dangling over the edge. Our narrator says he doesn't mind climbing down to collect any fallen sunglasses or sandals. And so, we get comfortable.

Looking through the glass bottom, the coral reefs are up close and personal. Sergeant majors, a fish named for its five black stripes, flash by as they wheel and turn around a reef. A young loggerhead turtle swims by and a nurse shark hangs out on the sand.

Coral reefs provide hiding and living places for fish and invertebrates. A coral reef grows very slowly. It is a living structure that keeps adding more polyps, individual polyps, thousands of them, to the colony.

Since 1990 the marine sanctuary has protected coral reefs, but their decline continues, in part because of rising water temperatures but also damage caused by boaters. Our boat narrator tells us something that I didn't realize—the entire Florida Keys is a coral cay archipelago. All those buildings are sitting on coral.

Sigh. It is time to turn around and head back to the dock. On this picture perfect day, I feel I am exactly where I should be, out on the water, inhaling salt air, viewing coral reefs, appreciating the awesome biodiversity of life above and below the waterline.

My boat tour

Date _____

Chapter 21

Transparensea Glass Bottomed Boat Tour

Duration: 2 hours

Cost: adult: $75 plus gratuity taxes and fees

Location: 77522 Overseas Highway, Islamorada, FL

Phone: 305-214-5277

Website: www.glassbottomtour.com

Good to know: Check in at least 15 minutes before departure time. Not handicapped accessible

The glass bottomed boat tour leaves from Robbie's Marina of Islamorada, a popular and crowded waterfront destination. Shops, bar, restaurant, pelicans waiting on a dock for handouts, food for sale to feed the tarpon, boat rentals, tours. Robbie's has it all.

I parked and then entered the maze of shops, weaved around, looking for boat tour signs, and asking directions. Found it. Checked in. Then onto the dock for boarding their new forty-six foot Seakeeper stabilized glass bottomed boat. The front end looks like the bow of a yacht, the rear is elongated with metal benches on either side of the glass viewing windows.

This is an ocean tour, into the Atlantic, visiting Cheeca Rocks Alligator Reef and Caloosa Rocks. Both are part of the Florida Keys National Marine Sanctuary. An ocean tour means there will be some rocking and rolling, something to keep in mind if prone to seasickness. To get to the first stop means the first half hour is full throttle forward, cruising out into the ocean to a coral reef.

On my trip that day there was a family with children about ages 7 and 9. They didn't mind the long boat ride to the first stop, but I can imagine parents with young children might want to take that long ride into consideration. Out of a two-hour tour, one hour is spent traveling to and from sites.

We stopped. Looking through the glass bottom we see live coral. Pretty amazing. Florida has America's only coral barrier reef. Corals are living organisms related to sea anemones and jellies. We're floating over hard corals, with lots of different shapes. Some are brain shaped, others rounded mounds, all grow very slowly. Small fish thread their way among the corals.

Corals are picky about where they live. A good life for them includes a solid structure for attachment, tropical or subtropical temperatures, clear water and moderate wave action. Their inability to move around, once attached to a substrate, makes them susceptible to threats like pollution and climate change.

Charlene, our narrator, relates that corals spawn according to phases of the moon and time of year. A group of divers, including Charlene, were underwater in late August hoping to see the event. Nothing happened for two hours. Then the lead diver rapped on his oxygen tank to get everyone's attention.

And it was happening. Clouds of sperm and eggs rose up from the hundreds of individual polyps in a coral colony. They will get together, sperm and egg, float around for a few days before attaching to anything. Corals are sessile, meaning they attach themselves to the ocean floor. Charlene said, hard as it is to believe, they can hear what is going on around them and look for signs of activity like a fish feeding at a coral reef. This where they want to be.

The captain starts up the motor and we move to the next spot some ten minutes away. Charlene releases some oatmeal into the water. Soon small fish are everywhere, easy to see through the viewing windows. A loggerhead turtle swims by on the surface, and we all get up to look over the side. Exciting! Meanwhile, down below, the boat floats over several big nurse sharks, looking like they are taking naps next to soft coral.

The hard coral we saw earlier has a skeleton made of calcium carbonate. The soft coral we're seeing now doesn't have that skeleton. They are more flexible and are usually in two forms: encrusting and branching. For sure the nurse sharks like being near soft coral.

The captain turns the boat around, puts the throttle forward and we head full speed ahead back to the dock at Robbie's.

My boat tour

Date _____

_____

_____

_____

_____

Acknowledgments

Gloria Collins suggested the title *Floating in Florida.* My editor, Sue Crawford, keeps me honest when it comes to style and accuracy. Kudos to all who came along on boat tours: Kate Singer, Ceil Bare, Sue Crawford, Dawn Finnerty, Lorrie Muldowney, Judy Johnson, Christopher Tobias. Two thumbs up to eagle eye readers: Judy Johnson, Mark Mathes, Jennifer Huber and Christopher Tobias. I am grateful to you all. Any mistakes are mine.

About the Author

Lucy Beebe Tobias is an award-winning author, blogger, journalist, photographer, and illustrator.

A former reporter for the New York Times Regional Group, Lucy's work included in-depth investigative reporting on the status of Florida panthers, Florida water issues and animal rights issues. She created an ongoing newspaper page called Discovery covering Florida environmental issues.

As the Authentic Florida expert for Visit Florida Lucy was the narrator for videos about Florida, including Apalachicola and the oyster debate, reenactments of civil war events and destination videos about undiscovered Florida. As the Authentic Florida expert she also blogged and spoke at Visit Florida events.

Lucy writes narrative non-fiction, looking at life and finding humor, beauty, and reasons for hope. Visit www.LucyTobias.com.

Lucy lives in Sarasota, Florida with one dog and two cats. All are rescues. Her back garden has native

plants, butterflies, birds, bees, and ponds overcrowded
with goldfish.

Bibliography

Alderson, Doug. *Florida's Rivers: A Celebration of Over 40 of the Sunshine State's Dynamic Waterways.* Sarasota: Pineapple Press, 2021.

Bass, Bob. *When Steamboats Reigned in Florida.* Gainesville: University of Florida Press, 2008.

Belleville, Bill. *A Journey on Florida's St. Johns River.* Athens: University of Georgia Press, 2001.

Boning, Charles. *Florida's Rivers.* Sarasota: Pineapple Press 2007.

Kilby, Rick. *Finding the Fountain of Youth: Ponce de Leon and Florida's Magical Waters.* Gainesville. University of Florida Press, 2013.

Livingston, Robert J. (editor). *The Rivers of Florida* (Ecological Studies, 83) . Springer, 1990.

The WPA Guide to Florida, New York: Pantheon Books, 1939.

Mueller, Edward A. *Along the St. Johns & Ocklawaha Rivers (Images of America: Florida).* Arcadia Press, 1999.

158

Poole, Leslie Kemp. *Tracing Florida Journeys Explorers, Travelers, and Landscapes Then and Now.* Gainesville. University of Florida Press, 2024.

Index

166